Parent's Concerns for their Unsaved Children

Several sermons on Proverbs 17:25,
published for the benefit of all, but especially
for the benefit of good parents and their children

by

Edward Lawrence, M. A.
(sometimes minister of the gospel at
Baschurch, in the county of Salop)

"Notwithstanding they hearkened not unto the voice of
their father, because the Lord would slay them."
1 Samuel 2:25

Edited by Dr. Don Kistler

Soli Deo Gloria Publications
. . . for instruction in righteousness . . .

Soli Deo Gloria Publications
A Division of Soli Deo Gloria Ministries, Inc.
P.O. Box 451, Morgan PA 15064
(412)221-1901/FAX 221-1902
www.SDGbooks.com

*

Parent's Concerns for their Unsaved Children was published in London in 1681 as *Parents' Groans Over Their Wicked Children.* This reprint, in which spelling, grammar, and formatting changes have been made,
Printed in the USA.

*

ISBN 1-57358-151-8

Library of Congress Cataloging-in-Publication Data

Lawrence, Edward, 1623-1695.
Parent's concerns for their unsaved children / by Edward Lawrence; edited by Don Kister.–[Rev. ed.].
p. cm.
Rev. ed. of: Parent's groans over their wicked children. 1681.
ISBN 1-57358-151-8 (softcover : alk. paper)
1. Parenting–Religious aspects–Christianity. I. Kistler, Don. II. Lawrence, Edward, 1623-1695. Parent's groans over their wicked children. III. Title.
BV4529.L278 2003
248.8'45–dc21

2003003544

Contents

To All Christian Parents

It is not only for the sake of myself and children, but also for the sake of you and yours, that I have published this little book; but I do so especially out of respect to the glory of God, that we may leave a seed to bless Him in this world when we are glorifying Him in the better world. It will cost you but a little money to buy it, and but a little time for you and your children to read it. If those of you who are able give to every one of your children one of these books, and likewise bestow some of them upon the children of the poor, this will be no advantage to me, and when you come to give your account, will be no loss to you. I am a lover of children, and have often lifted up my heart in prayer to God for them where I have seen them. I wish this may be a blessing to you and to them; pray that we may leave that religion which came originally from the Father of Jesus Christ, and is revealed to us in the Scriptures, to our posterity, and that they may have hearts to live according to the rules and principles of it more than we have done. Farewell.

Your Servant for Jesus' sake,

Edward Lawrence
June 6, 1681

To My Beloved Children

Deborah, Samuel, Edward, John, Thomas,
Elizabeth, Mary, Benjamin, and Nathanael
(and to all the children of Christian parents)

My Dear Children:

I am sensible of my unworthiness and unfitness to be seen in print; it is now more than twenty years since, by the power and goodness of God, I was unexpectedly rescued from the jaws of death, which was the reason I then published that little book called *Christ's Power Over Bodily Diseases.* And I would never have been the author of a book of this title had not two of you (but especially one) made me the father of fools.

I shall here say no more particularly to you two but that sound repentance and the fruits thereof, in a settled reformation of life, will yet be your glory and my joy; but if you hate to be reformed (God forbid) I shall mourn till I die for the loss of children, but you will be tormented forever for the loss of God.

Children, I do not have the things of this world to leave you. I acknowledge the wisdom of God in not judging me fit to be entrusted with these things; but it's enough for us if we can call God our own, though we cannot call the riches of the world our own. Some of you with comfort remember how we have often worshipped God together in singing with delight those words from Psalm 37:16–20: "A little that a righteous man hath is better than the riches of many wicked."

I here leave you this letter of the counsel and advice of your aged, loving, and faithful father, who sees death looking him and you in the face, and beholds the Judge before the door. This will speak to you when death has silenced me; it speaks the same thing which God, Christ, and your own consciences speak to you; and it speaks to you (as it were) in the hearing of the world.

Put a true value on your own beings, for you cannot love God and Christ if you do not love yourselves; you are of that kind of creature who is made much higher than all other visible creatures, and but a little lower than the angels. You are capable to know, choose, love and delight in God, to speak of Him, and to entertain yourselves continually with Him. You are of those creatures in whose happiness God glorifies all His perfections. He made this world for man. He commanded His only-begotten Son to sacrifice Himself for man, and sent Him to be born, to live, to die, to rise again, and to intercede in heaven for man. He has revealed all the truths of the Christian religion for the good of man; and therefore you should think it greater madness to sell your precious souls and bodies to the devil and your lusts for the short and dirty pleasures of sin than to sell a purse of gold or a cabinet full of jewels for a bag of chaff or cherry stones. You should account it beneath you to give yourselves to anyone but God.

Know that as your beings are great, so your happiness or misery will be very great. Riches or poverty, sickness or health, this present life or the death that deprives you of it, are things too little to make you blessed or miserable; all the curses of God or the blessings of the gospel will be upon you presently; and you can neither live like men nor like Christians until you know what it is to be favored or damned, and what it is to lose or enjoy God.

That you may escape the wrath that is set before you, and obtain the glory set before you instead, let it be your chief end and interest to know, honor, and enjoy God. Use the creatures as His witnesses to testify and declare the being and glory of God to you; for God has not only made and appointed them to fill your hearts with food and gladness, but also that in the use of them you may feel, find, and fill your souls with God. But especially behold the glory of God as He is presented to you in the glass of the Scriptures, that He may have that name in your hearts which He has in His Word.

Present Him to your souls as God over all, blessed forever, so that you may conclude that He who is so infinitely good as to be His own happiness is sufficient to make you happy. And that this God may be your eternal life and happiness, you must know and behold His glory in the face of Jesus Christ, who is the image of the invisible God, the brightness of His glory, and the express image of His person; therefore behold His glory as the Father of such a Son, and as the Lord of such a Servant, for Jesus Christ is the Lord's Christ (Luke 2:26). Christ is God's (1 Corinthians 3:23), and executes His office of a Mediator in obedience to the will and to the glory of God the Father, whose glory you may behold in His calling Him to such a high office, in His accomplishing Him for the execution thereof, in prospering Him and making Him successful in His whole work, in giving Him such a blessed seed, in making Him victorious over all His enemies, and in rewarding Him for His great service and obedience. So then, according to the intent of Scriptures forenamed, you must labor to get such a sight of the glory of God shining upon you in the face of Jesus Christ as will make an impression of His image in your souls.

Therefore loathe and abhor sin, which is against the glory of God, and which is the only evil that can make you lose such a glorious God.

For this reason be convinced of the vanity of this world, which is but a poor thing when the glory of God shines on your souls; for you will be most blessed in Him when this world shall be dissolved and passed away.

Let this make Jesus Christ glorious and acceptable to you, whose office and work it is to redeem you from all sin and misery, and to make you blessed forever in the likeness and enjoyment of this glorious God.

Let this also cause you to endeavor to fill all persons with the great name of God and Christ, so that you may gain for them all the hearts, love, and service you can; and therefore in all your company let God and Christ have your good word.

Know that to love and delight in God is the best employment for the days of your youth. God is much concerned for young persons. The Proverbs of Solomon are written to give to the young man knowledge and discretion (Proverbs 1:4), and one great use of the Word of God is to teach young men to cleanse their way (Psalm 119:9). Young men, maidens, and children are called upon to praise the name of the Lord (Psalm 148:12–13). We find many mourning with holy Augustine that they loved God too late, but none complaining that they loved Him too soon. As young as you are, in heaven and hell, it's better to be a young child of God than a young child of the devil. Young saints are the glory of God, the fullness and accomplishment of Christ, the joy of angels, the security and support of religion, the crown of their parents, and the blessing of their generation.

Fill your time with the fruits of the Spirit; see that your hearts are filled with grace, and then your days will be filled with fruit. Always be receiving Christ, and resigning yourselves to Him. Feel your hearts continually laying hold on eternal life, and live as if you were always running to heaven. Spend every day so that you may lie down in peace at night, and that the Lord's Day may be pleasant, death gainful, and eternity glorious.

Improve God's ordinances of worship; feel your view of baptism always fresh and strong upon you; feel the difference between the Lord's Day and other days. See that the Word preached is mixed with faith and engrafted in your hearts, so that it kills your sins and reforms your lives. Pray continually, and in that duty see that you are with the spirits of children with your Father in heaven. Let all your affairs pass through praying hearts. And reckon all your own which you sincerely pray for. Sing psalms, as those that make God your song and joy, and as if you were sensible that you are in the gates of heaven, ready to enter therein, to join with that world of blessed angels and saints in admiring and praising God. When you come to the Lord's Supper, see all that is presented to you, receive all that is offered, and do all that is commanded you.

Be faithful to the truth, and then you need not be afraid of yourselves or of any other. This is your greatest safety, and you may then feel the ground firm under you, and may say with David in Psalm 26:12, "My foot standeth in an even place." And if you are called to suffer, choose it rather than sin; and seeing men cannot kill your souls, let not the fear of them make you destroy them yourselves.

Decline evil company; do not go with them to hell who will not go with you to heaven. But if you are called into such company, feel yourselves with God while you are with them, and carry it as those who are sensible that there is a God in the place. Exercise those graces which are contrary to and condemn their sins. Be humble with the proud, meek with the angry, and loving with the malicious, so that they may be reproved by your graces and that you may not be defiled by their sins.

Labor to be a blessing to all persons; let men see that in you for which they may have cause to love and praise God. Bear all wrongs, but do none; do what in you lies to make all persons holy and joyful, but make none sinful, angry, or sad. Forgive all, but let none have need to forgive you. Exercise their love, but do not by your sins exercise their patience. Give all cause to bless God for you, but give no cause to any to wish they had never known you.

Dread debts; do not unnecessarily bring yourselves under the bondage of debtors. Look upon it as more just and honorable to beg than to borrow, if you are not likely to pay, unless in that case you plainly acquaint the lender with your condition so that he may know what adventure he makes. And when you are able, pay seasonably, fully, and thankfully. I would have none to lend to any children of mine without first advising with me, unless they are in a hopeful way of trade. And my advice to such of you is that you be afraid of being too much trusted. For it's often seen that they who go to the length of their credit are injurious to others and prove bankrupt to themselves.

Abhor lying. This is a sin which is an abomination to the Lord, whom you should always please. It is contrary to the divine nature, which is in everyone who is born of God (Ephesians 4:24). It is an abuse of your tongues, which should be your glory; for the use of your tongues is to express your minds. But in a lie your minds and thoughts contradict your words. It is a wrong to others whom you would have believe you, when you do not believe yourselves. It makes you unfit for human society, for who will converse with those whom they cannot believe. You hereby rot your names, for a liar is one of the worst characteristics of the devil of hell; you destroy your bodies and souls forever, for "all liars shall have their part in the lake of fire and brimstone, which is the second death."

Do not dare to steal. Take nothing from any person but what you can say you received from the hand of God, can praise Him for it, and can comfortably beg His blessing upon it. Kill those lusts which you would feed with the fruit of other men's labors. Consider that when you are tempted to this sin of theft, you are tempted to bring a curse on your estates and persons, to thrust a dagger into your father's heart, and to hasten yourselves to an untimely and shameful death, and a tormenting eternity.

Deride and jeer no persons. Let your jests be harmless, and do not make yourselves the fools of your company. But while you are cheerful as men and women, do not lose the favor of Christians.

Do not haunt taverns or alehouses. Do not go into

such places but when God calls you. Stay no longer than He will stay with you, and do nothing there but what you shall have cause to bless God for when you come away.

Be thankful to them who have shown mercy and kindness to me and you. Pray for them; inquire how it is with their posterity, and, as you are capable, do them good. Remember Proverbs 27:10: "Thy own friend, and thy father's friend, forsake not."

Forgive all who have done me wrong, and pray to God not to visit it on them or their posterity. You know I have had hard measure from some, and I know that I have stood before God to speak good for them and to turn away His wrath from them.

As for you who are or may be hereafter set up for yourselves in a way of trade, my counsel to you is this: See that your persons are upright with God, that you may have a Scripture-right to the promises of the life that now is and of that which is to come, which is to be preferred before the best estate in the world. Pray to God for His blessing, and see every customer as sent from Him, and love them as yourselves. Let all who deal with you have cause to say that they deal with the members of Jesus Christ.

And for you who are or may be apprentices, my counsel and command to you is this: Let those Scriptures dwell in your hearts which teach you your duty and encourage you therein (Ephesians 5:5–8; Colossians 3:22–25; Titus 2:9–10; 1 Peter 2:18–21). Commit these to memory, and bless God that He condescends to be a teacher of servants. Be content with your present condition, which may be the easiest time of your whole age. Do not be apt to find fault, for that will make you uneasy to yourselves and to the family. Let all your words and looks and actions be such as witness that in your hearts you honor your masters and mistresses, and Christ in them. Bear correction patiently, though you are wronged. The sufferings of Christ are set before you as your pattern herein. Pray daily for your masters and their families, for you ought to improve all your interest in God for their good. Pray to God to fit you for your calling, that He who teaches the husbandman to plow and sow (Isaiah 28:26) may teach you herein.

To conclude, love one another according to all the obligations that are upon you, but never put it in the power of any one to undo the other.

Kill all lustings after the honors, riches, or pleasures of the world. Remember I have told you that as love fulfills all the law of God, so lust fulfills the law of the devil. I will say no more. Choose Him for your Father who cannot die. And as Mr. [Robert] Bolton said to his children, so say I to you, "Do not dare to meet me at the day of judgment in an unregenerate state."

Your loving and faithful father,

Edward Lawrence
June 6, 1681

Chapter 1

"A foolish son is a grief to his father, and bitterness to her that bare him." Proverbs 17:25

The Text Opened

It is one great argument of the vanity of this world that we may be spoiled of all that is dear to us under the sun by the sins of other men. A common and sad instance of this is that the comforts of godly parents here are very much at the will and pleasure of their own children. For had a good man all other delights that the creature can yield, washed his steps in butter and dipped his foot in oil, nay, suppose he had all the pleasures of godliness that are ordinarily attained in this life, yet he will be a man of sorrow if a wicked child makes him the father of a fool.

This doleful case is presented to us in this text which I have chosen for the subject of this discourse, so that I may duly affect my own and others' hearts with this great calamity.

In the text two things are clearly set before us:

A case taken for granted, and that is that godly parents often have foolish children.

The misery of that case is expressed, that is, that such children are a grief to their fathers, and bitterness to the mothers who bore them.

The Explication of the Text

A foolish son is a wicked and ungodly son or daughter. It is usual in this book of the Proverbs that both sexes are intended when but one is expressed. Wicked children think themselves wise, wiser than their parents, masters, or ministers; for vain man would be wise, though he is like a wild ass's colt (Job 11:12). But all the devil's children are fools; for he who will obey and imitate the devil, who is a murderer of all his own children, and will not obey and imitate Christ, who is the Redeemer and Savior of all His children, I may say of him in the words of a wise woman, " 'Fool' is his name, and folly is with him."

"A foolish son is a grief to his father. . . ." By father and mother in the text, I understand a godly father and mother, who are most affected with this case. Some render the word translated "grief" to mean anger or indignation, and both grief and anger are intended, for a foolish son makes his good father both angry and sad.

"And bitterness to her that bare him," that is, to his good mother, called "her that bare him" to aggravate the mother's misery and the child's sin. It cannot but torment the good mother to think that she did—with so much sickness, pain, and sorrow—bear and bring forth one who proves to be a child of the devil, and is likely to be a firebrand of hell. And it is a great aggravation of the child's sins to embitter the life of her who was a means of life to him, and to hasten that womb to the worms which with such pangs and throws brought him into the world.

The text will be further opened in the following discourse, which I shall reduce to these three headings:

1. It is ordinary for godly parents to have wicked and ungodly children.

2. This is a very great calamity to these godly parents.

3. The use.

1. It is ordinary for godly parents to have wicked and ungodly children. This is implied in the text. And I may say of this what Solomon speaks of another case in Ecclesiastes 6:1: "It is an evil which I have seen under the sun," and it is common among men.

In the handling of this, I shall:

- Give some characters of godly parents.
- Give some characters of ungodly children.
- Give you several instances for the confirmation of it.

I shall only give you two main characters of godly parents: They are conscientiously careful for their preservation, and they are conscientiously careful for the eternal happiness and salvation of their children.

First, they are conscientiously careful for the preservation of the natural lives of their children, as trees support and feed the branches that grow out of themselves. As it is natural to brute beasts to defend and keep their own young, so nature itself teaches and inclines parents to defend and preserve, and provide for the fruit of their own bodies. And to this end, they supply them with food, raiment, and medicine, and make them fit them for their callings, and seasonably provide for them meet yoke-fellows, and in every way take care that they neither perish or be made miserable. But godly parents, in whom natural affections are sanctified and improved by grace, do all these out of a principle of godliness, as persons who have to do with God herein; they do it in a sense of their dependence on God, pray for daily bread to feed their children, and are thankful when they feel it come warmly from their Father in heaven. They do it in obedience and faithfulness to God, and with a design that their children may live to be born of God, to be a blessing to this world, and be blessed in the other world. As for those unnatural monsters, who feed their lusts with that which should maintain their children, they are so far from being godly parents that they are worse than infidels in not providing for their families, and are like the devil, who (as I said) is a murderer of his own children.

Second, they are conscientiously careful for the eternal happiness and salvation of their children, for their natural affections being now sanctified work in them for the spiritual good and happiness of their children. Proverbs 4:3–5: "I was my father's son, tender and only beloved in the sight of my mother." Solomon was his father's and mother's darling; their love ran out exceedingly upon this son, and he tells us which way their love and kindness was expressed: "He taught me also, and said unto me, 'Get wisdom, get understanding.' " He tells us also how the affections of his good mother worked in Proverbs 31:2–3: "What my son? And what the son of my womb? And what the son of my vows?" The son of her womb was the son of her vows, whom she had devoted to God. Those parents who have known both states, the state of wrath and the state of grace, and have experimentally felt what it is to pass from death to life, and from the kingdom of Satan into the kingdom of God, cannot but desire that the same change be wrought upon their children. And as they who love themselves with a holy love take God for their eternal life and happiness, Christ for their Redeemer to redeem them from all evil and to bring them to this happiness; and the Spirit for their Sanctifier, to fit them for this happiness, so they who love their children with this holy love will desire and endeavor that they be partakers with them of the same happiness.

I proceed to give you three characteristics of ungodly children:

First, they are such children as will not be subject to the authority of their parents. The reverence of children to their parents is so incorporated into the whole body of religion that all religion is in vain without it. This fully appears in Leviticus 19:3: "Ye shall fear every man his mother, and his father, and keep my Sabbaths. I am the Lord your God." Observe, this duty is here joined with keeping the Lord's Sabbaths, wherein religion always very much consisted. But it's often seen that disobedient children are great profaners of the Lord's Day; they are always bad, but usually worst on that day. And some of them may remember that their first breaking out into scandalous sins was on the Lord's Day. We are here further taught that this duty of reverence to parents is joined with all religion to God; for, God says in effect, "It is in vain for any to pretend to call me their Lord and their God if they do not fear their parents." And therefore wicked children are numbered among the worst sinners. Ezekiel 22:7: "In thee have they set light by father and mother." They vilified and despised them, and made nothing of them. Such break all the bonds of religion, and many hasten through a shameful and untimely death into a dreadful and tormenting eternity, whose wickedness first began in scorning and despising their parents.

Second, they are such children as will not obey the commands of their parents. The godly commands of parents are the means which God has appointed, and often blesses, to make the children godly. Genesis 18:19: "I know Abraham, that he will command his children, and his household after him, and they shall keep the way of the Lord to do justice and judgment." And God commands all children to obey all the holy and lawful commands of their parents in Ephesians 6:1: "Children obey your parents in the Lord, for this is right." It is the parents' right that their children should obey them, and it is God's right that they should obey them in the Lord. And this, says the apostle in Colossians 3:20, is well-pleasing to the Lord. So that those children neither fear provoking God nor care to please Him who will not obey their parents. And so they are children of their parents' sorrow, and of God's wrath.

Third, they are such children as are unthankful to their parents. The apostle tells us in 1 Timothy 5:4 that it is good and acceptable before God for children to requite their parents. And they have great things for which they should labor to requite their godly parents: for all their care, cost, and pains to keep them alive, and for all their diligence and faithfulness in endeavoring to make them blessed; and all the requital which the poor parents desire is that their children would but love and obey God and not damn themselves. But these ungodly children are so far from requiting them that, like so many dogs and lions, they tear in pieces the hearts and bowels of their tender parents.

I now come to confirm that it is ordinary for godly

parents to have ungodly children. And for this end, I shall give you some instances recorded in Scripture. Then I shall cite several cases wherein this is verified.

I shall give you four examples recorded in Scripture for the confirmation hereof.

EXAMPLE 1. Adam and Eve were both godly parents; and therefore in that first evangelical promise (Genesis 3:15) we have notice of the two great parties in the world; the one was the woman and her seed, the second is the serpent and his seed, and of the enmity between them. And though there is only mention made of the woman, yet the man is also included, so that by the woman and her seed we are to understand Adam and Eve (and Christ and His Church), and by the serpent and his seed are meant the devil and all the devil's children. And forasmuch as we find Adam and Eve of the same party with Christ and His church, and in enmity with the devil and his seed, we conclude Adam and Eve to be godly persons and godly parents. Moreover we find in Genesis 4 that they brought up their children in that religion, and to worship God in the use of those ordinances which He had then instituted as a means of their salvation. These two people were the first-fruits of Christ, the first persons who ever entered into the covenant of grace; and Christ might say to them, as Jacob said to Reuben in Genesis 49:3, "Ye are my first-born, my might, and the beginning of my strength." At first the whole Church of God was only in these two persons, and yet these are the parents of that cursed and bloody Cain. And I shall observe three things in this history that render this case very doleful:

One, Eve was exceedingly glad for the birth of Cain. Some are of opinion that she thought she had brought forth the promised Messiah, and that made her break out with joy, saying, "I have gotten a man from the Lord" (Genesis 4:1). And yet this is he of whom the apostle speaks in 1 John 3:12: "He was of that wicked one," meaning the devil. This is a common case: parents are exceedingly glad for the birth of a child, and call their friends and neighbors to rejoice with them; and yet that sweet and pleasant babe proves to be the greatest torment to their parents which ever they met with in their whole lifetime!

Two, consider Cain's crime: he barbarously murdered his own brother. Genesis 4:8: "Cain rose up against Abel, his brother, and slew him." He did not consider how this would grieve the heart of his good father and mother, nor that he was the elder brother and therefore ought to have nourished the life of the younger, and to have been a pattern of holiness and love to him; neither did he consider that he hated and murdered not only a brother, but also a holy child of God, and for that which he ought to have honored and loved him: because his brother's works were righteous. And he did not consider how his brother's blood would cry to God for vengeance against him. No bonds, arguments, or reasons will prevail with ungodly children.

Three, consider the dreadful judgment of God upon both Cain and his posterity. God's judgment on his soul was so dreadful that he desperately cried out in Genesis 4:13, "My punishment is greater than I can bare." He was cast out of the favor of God, excommunicated from the church, and all his posterity were excluded from communion therewith. They are called the sons and daughters of men (in opposition to the sons of God), and at last all perished in the deluge of waters.

And yet, I say, this bloody and cursed monster was the son, the eldest son of the two first godly parents that ever were in the world.

EXAMPLE 2. The first example was the first godly man in the old world, as the ages before the flood are called in 2 Peter 2:5. This example is Noah, the best man in the new world after the flood. Noah had a great character, as we read in Genesis 6:8–9: "Noah found grace in the eyes of the Lord. Noah was a just man, and perfect in his generations." When all the earth was debauched and corrupt (Genesis 6:11–12), yet was Noah just and upright, and walked with God. It is he who is called in 2 Peter 2:5 "a preacher of righteousness." It is he who was so much in the favor of God that he and his family were singled out to be preserved in the ark when all the world besides were drowned and perished in the waters. Yet this holy Noah was the father of that wicked Ham, whom all "the waters of Noah" (as the Scripture calls that deluge) were not effectual to cure his wickedness. but Ham went into the ark a wicked man, and came out wicked, insomuch that his own holy father was inspired by a prophetic spirit to curse both his son and posterity. And the crime mentioned in Genesis 9:22–25 was his irreverence and disrespect to his father.

EXAMPLE 3. Isaac was a holy Patriarch, who so greatly feared God that his son Jacob gives God that honorable name (Genesis 31:42) "the fear of Isaac," meaning "the God whom Isaac feared." Yet he and the good mother Rebekah were the parents of wicked Esau, whom God is said to hate (Romans 9:13). I know we read in Genesis 25:28 that Isaac loved Esau, but we see that children may be greatly beloved of their parents and yet be abhorred and cursed by God.

EXAMPLE 4. David is called "a man after God's own heart," whom God raised up to be king of Israel. He was a penman of a considerable part of the holy Scriptures, and such an eminent type of Christ that Christ Himself is often called "David" in Scripture. Yet he was the tender father of that wicked Absalom, who bloodily murdered his brother Amnon, and miserably and shamefully died in treason and rebellion against his royal father, whose bitter lamentation is yet in our ears. 2 Samuel 18:33: "O my son Absalom, my son, my son Absalom! Would God I had died for thee; O Absalom my son, my son!"

Now I shall give you four cases wherein this is often verified.

CASE 1. Those children who are most beloved of their parents often prove to be the most wicked children. Absalom was David's darling, insomuch that although he set his whole kingdom in a flame, and constrained his father to flee for his life, yet when David sent out his army to suppress that rebellion he gave this charge to his commanders in the audience of the soldiers: "Deal gently for my sake with the young man, even with Absalom" (2 Samuel 18:5).

CASE 2. It often happens that the children who have most of their parents' love and delight, and whose looks and talk they are most taken with, of whom they are most apt to boast, with whom they are most unwilling to part, and in whom they promise themselves most content and pleasure, often prove to be the greatest scourge and torment to their parents; for it is not the love of the godly parents, but the love of God that makes children holy and happy.

CASE 3. This is often the sad case of some holy ministers of the Word. I know it is a popish and peevish humor in some to say that ministers' children never do well; indeed, everything of ministers is most exposed to the observation of people, and therefore the wickedness of their children is most observed and talked of. But the holy, learned and in everyway prosperous and blessed seed of divers godly ministers is sufficient to confute and shame the ignorance of people herein; and yet it is true that many godly ministers in all ages have groaned under this sad calamity. Eli was a holy priest of God, but his two sons were devils incarnate, monsters of men, scandalous, sacrilegious and adulterous sons of Belial, as appears in 1 Samuel 2. And it is no rare thing that the prayers, studies, sermons, and examples of many good ministers are often made successful to bring others to heaven while they can by no means restrain their own children from running to hell. Their own children often make them do the work of their ministry with grief when often the children of drunkards, worldlings, and whoremongers will be their crown and glory in the day of the Lord Jesus.

This is often true when both parents are godly. Indeed, when either father or mother is wicked, no marvel if the children are hardened in their sins by their examples. But it is usually seen that when children have both the instruction of the father and also the law of the mother, and when they cry to all the ministers and Christians about them to help them by their prayers and counsels to save their children, yet all this may not prevail. And then the holy father and mother can scarcely keep one another's hearts from being broken by their stubborn and disobedient children.

CASE 4. The children of godly parents often prove

wicked when God sanctifies, blesses, and saves the children of ungodly parents. We see sometimes trees of righteousness growing in the families of the wicked, while briars and thorns grow up in the families of the righteous. We read in Matthew 1 that Ahaz, a very wicked king, begat holy Hezekiah, and good Hezekiah begat Manasseh, who was an idolater of the highest rate, a witch, and such a bloody murderer that the Chronicles of his reign tells us (2 Kings 21:16) that he "shed innocent blood very much, until he had filled Jerusalem from one end to the other" (though afterwards he is set forth to be the greatest pattern of the grace of God in the Old Testament, as Paul is in the New Testament). It is no new sight to see children of the best saints on the way to hell, and children of atheists and persecutors on the way to heaven. Nay, though some parents persecute their own children for loving and fearing God, yet they cannot debauch them, while all endeavors of godly parents may not prevail to make their children hate sin and love God. This is one of the saddest instances of that great mystery of providence mentioned in Ecclesiastes 8:14: "There be just men, to whom it happeneth according to the work of the wicked; again, there be wicked men to whom it happeneth according to the work of the righteous."

Chapter 2

The Calamity of Godly Parents Having Unsaved Children

It is a very great calamity to godly parents to have wicked and ungodly children. "A foolish son (says the Proverbs text) is a grief to his father, and bitterness to her that bare him." To the same purpose is Proverbs 17:21: "He that begetteth a fool doeth it to his sorrow, and the father of a fool hath no joy." A foolish son dampens all his joy. And Proverbs 19:13: "A foolish son is the calamity of his father."

I shall set forth the greatness of this trouble by these eight particulars:

1. By the matter of these parents' grief.
2. By the passions that this calamity moves and affects.
3. By comparing this with other afflictions, and showing how this exceeds them.
4. By showing that this makes these parents do all their work with grief and sorrow.
5. By showing that this embitters all their other comforts.
6. By the sad concomitants of it.
7. By the several aggravations of it.
8. By instancing in some cases wherein this calamity is more grievous.

1. The matter of these parents' grief is very sad, as appears in these seven things:

First, their children are so defiled and debauched with sin, which is so loathsome to these holy parents. It vexed the righteous soul of Lot to see and hear the filthy conversation of the beastly Sodomites. How grievous then must it be to these godly parents to see and hear the filthiness of their own dear children. It is a grievous thing to a man who loves God, godliness, and souls to see a drunkard staggering in the streets, or to hear any man blaspheming and reproaching his Maker and Redeemer. But none can tell but those who feel it what a sad spectacle it is to sober and godly parents see their own children drunk, or how it torments them to hear their own children lying and blaspheming God and His saints.

Second, their children are the children of the devil, under the power of Satan, ridden by him, and carried captive by him at his will. It was a lamentable case of that good mother who came to Christ in Matthew 15:22, saying, "Have mercy upon me, O Lord, Thou Son of David, my daughter is grievously vexed with a devil." Yet this was not her daughter's sin, but only her great affliction. But how doleful is it to these parents, who have renounced the devil themselves and live in continual warfare with him, to see the hearts and mouths and lives of the children whom they have devoted to God filled and possessed with the devil, whose children they are and whose lusts they will do. If the devil tempts the parents, their own graces will resist and overcome his temptations; but they cannot secure their children from being overcome, and from falling into the condemnation of the devil. With sad hearts they see the lion of hell running away with the lambs of their flock, and cannot recover them.

Third, their children are under the wrath and curse of God; it sadly affected the father of that lunatic son, mentioned in Matthew 17:15, to see his son fall often into the fire and into the water. How he would screech at such a sight, and cry, "Ah, my dear child will be burned! My child will be drowned!" But much more terrible is it to these parents, who know the terrors of the Lord, to know that their children have cut off the entail of the covenant of grace, and are every moment ready to fall into the hands of the living God! When such parents are, with faith, reading the curses of God's law, how it cuts them to the heart to think that they are then reading their children's doom!

Fourth, their children are under those black characteristics which are given in Scripture to ungodly men; for the faith of these parents makes all persons have that name in their hearts which they have in the Word. And as God is no respecter of persons, so faith, so far as it prevails, does not respect the persons of any, no, not of a man's own children. But because they are more under their notice and observation than others, and because they are more concerned for them, therefore the deeper impressions these characteristics make on their hearts. So this is the misery of these parents is that, while they look on persons through the glass of the Scriptures, and see many to be the jewels, treasures, children, heirs of God, and the glorious bride and spouse of Christ, they must judge their own wicked children to be a generation of vipers, serpents, dogs, swine, lions, bears, and wolves, as God calls them in His Word.

Fifth, the anger and displeasure of God appears so much against these good parents here; indeed, the sense of their own folly must make them justify God in this sharp correction, and cause them to say with Solomon, "As it is meet that there be a whip for the horse, and a bridle for the ass, so it is that there be a rod for the fool's back" (Proverbs 26:3). But this is very grievous that God should correct them with a scourge made of their own bowels, and should chasten a blessed father with a cursed child. His holy anger must be acknowledged herein; for when the child despises his father, God Himself justly spits in the father's face.

Sixth, the shame and disgrace which comes to them hereby. Proverbs 19:26: "He that wasteth his father, and chaseth away his mother, is a son that causeth shame." Everyone will be ready to reflect upon their parents and to say, "Surely these children were never taught to serve God, who so sacrifice themselves to the service of the devil."

Seventh, both parents are deeply affected for the trouble and misery that comes hereby to one another; their love to and sympathy with one another makes the burden of both more uneasy. The good father is not only troubled with a wicked child, but also for the bitterness and sorrow of his wife. And the good mother is not only troubled with the wicked child, but also for the grief of her husband. The mother's heart bleeds to see the tears, and to hear the groans of the afflicted father, and cries out, "Oh, what a child I brought forth, that so deprives me of the comfort of a loving husband, and is likely to break his heart, and to make me a desolate and disconsolate widow!" The father mourns to see the tears and sad countenance, and to hear the groans of the distressed mother. And he is ready to cry out, "Woe is me, that the child of my bowels is destroying the wife of my bosom!" And yet these hard-hearted children are not affected herewith. Let the parents sigh, they will sing; let the parents weep and mourn, they will rant and roar, and care no more to break their parents' hearts than to break a tobacco pipe. They will not abate a lie, a curse, or cup to save the lives of their tender parents.

2. The greatness of this calamity appears by the passions in the parents which are moved and affected hereby. I shall only give you three: fear, anger, and sorrow.

Fear. This is a troublesome passion, and godly parents are never void of fear of their wicked children. They are afraid that everyone who knocks at the door, and that every post, and every friend who comes to visit them, brings them some sad tidings of their disobedient children. I shall amplify this by giving three great evils which such parents are greatly perplexed with the fear of.

They are afraid lest their children are in the practice of some great sins. This was Job's fear when his children were feasting together (Job 1:5). Job said, "It may be my sons have sinned and cursed God in their hearts." Their children are seldom out of their sight, but the good parents are in fear of this. They know their children are always exposed to the devil's temptations, to the snares of the world, to the allurements of evil company, that their corrupt hearts are set to comply with all of those, and that they have provoked God to give them up to their own lusts. And therefore they are in continual fear lest these poor children are lying, swearing, cursing, whoring, or are drunk, defiling, debauching and destroying themselves and others.

They are in fear lest some heavy judgment of God will befall them in this life. And thus David, when his son Absalom was in the head of a high rebellion against his father, and the battle was to be fought with the rebels, was fearful lest his son should then perish in his sins. These parents know that their poor children are out of God's way, and are, as birds wandering from the nest (Proverbs 27:8), are exposed to all manner of danger. They know what the Word threatens against them, and what fearful instances there are of the vengeance of God upon disobedient children. And therefore they are in fear lest their sins should bring them to some untimely and shameful death.

They are in fear of their eternal damnation. They are sensible that their children are children of wrath, and live in those sins for which the wrath of God comes on the children of disobedience. And these parents believe what hell is; for as faith in the promises is the substance of things hoped for, so faith, as it believes the threatenings, is the substance of things feared. And therefore they cannot but tremble to think that their dear lambs, whom they so tenderly nourished and cherished, are in danger every moment of being cast into the fire that is prepared for devils.

Anger. Anger is another passion that is moved in godly parents because of the wickedness of their children. And this is troublesome, for a man is never out of trouble while he is in anger. And the more the wills of these parents are bent to have their children godly, the more are they displeased and provoked to anger by their sins. They are angry to see them provoke that God whom they themselves are so careful to please, to see them destroying their precious souls which they are laboring to save, and to see them waste those estates on their filthy lusts which they have gotten by their care and labor and prayers. They cannot but think of them with anger, speak of them with anger, and look at them with anger. And thus their children, who should be their delight and pleasure, are a continual cross and vexation to them.

Sorrow. They are deeply affected with grief and sorrow for the wickedness of their children; the parents' graces cause them to mourn for their children's sins. Their saving knowledge makes their hearts bleed to see their children scorn and despise that glory which they see in God and Christ. And while they by faith are feeding on Christ, it grieves them to see their children feeding themselves with the dirty pleasures of sin. Their love to God makes them groan that their children love sin, the worst evil, and hate God, the chief good.

3. I will now show the greatness of this calamity by comparing it with other troubles and showing how this exceeds them. I shall compare this one with four other troubles:

First, this is a greater calamity than to be without children; so that if God had said of those parents, as he said of the man in Jeremiah 22:30, "Write ye this man, and this woman childless," the punishment would not have been so great as to be afflicted with wicked children. Such parents may say with our Savior in another case (Luke 23:29), "Blessed are the barren, and the wombs that never bare, and the paps which never gave suck." As it is better to have no herbs in your gardens than to have only stinking weeds that cumber the ground, and better to have no beasts on your ground than a company of foxes and wolves, so it is better to have no children than to have only such who are the continual shame and plague and torment of their parents.

Second, it is a greater misery than to have diseased or deformed children. It indeed is a sore affliction to be the parents of sick, blind, lame, or deformed children, because such children are naturally disabled to do that service to God, their generation, and their parents which otherwise they might do. But this is not so grievous as to have wicked children; for they who are most diseased and uncomely are often called to be the blessed and glorious children, heirs of God, and the amiable and beautiful bride and spouse of Christ, when all wicked children are the filthy and loathsome children of the devil.

Third, this is more grievous than the death of children. I know it is matter of deep sorrow when parents may say with the tender Patriarch (Genesis 42:36: "Joseph is not, and Simeon is not"), "My son is dead, and is not; and my dear daughter is dead, and is not." But this kind of sorrow is not lasting; the impression of it usually does, and should, wear off. But wicked children are constant troubles to their parents, and cause them to say with the Psalmist, "My days are spent with grief, and my years with sighing" (Psalm 31:10).

Fourth, this calamity is greater than persecution from wicked men, though that is also very grievous, insomuch that Paul, a man of a great spirit, was so affected herewith that he solemnly beseeched the Roman Christians (Romans 15:30) for the Lord Jesus' sake, and for the love of the Spirit, that they would strive together with him in prayer to God for him, to deliver him from persecuting men. It is a sad case to be smitten and wounded in our names by lying and slanderous tongues. David (and Christ in him) tells us in Psalm 69:20 that reproach had broken his heart. It is sad for the jewels of God to be accounted and used as the sink and toilets of the world, to have our estates wasted and spoiled, to be exposed to beggary and want, to be dragged from our healthful and pleasant habitations and families, to be cast among rogues and thieves into nasty and loathsome prisons, and to have our innocent and precious blood shed by barbarous men. But all this is not as grievous as to be tormented by wicked children, for in those other cases we are distressed by the sins of our enemies, and if so, as David says in Psalm 55:12, we could have borne it. But in this case we are afflicted by the sins of our own children, and may say with David, when he was reviled by Shimei, "Behold, my son which came forth of my bowels, seeketh my life; how much more may this Benjamite do it?" (2 Samuel 16:11). It is a far greater torment to have the children of our own bowels tear and break our hearts than to be destroyed by merciless enemies.

4. The greatness of this calamity is seen in that it causes these good parents to do all their work with sorrow. I shall instance three sorts of works which they do in the bitterness of their souls: natural, civil, and religious works. He who has a wicked child on his heart does all these with a sad heart.

These parents do their natural works with sorrow. They are fed with the bread of tears, and drink their tears in great measure, as the Psalmist speaks in another case (Psalm 80:5). And as it is said in the prayer regarding the afflicted (Psalm 102:9), they eat ashes like bread and mingle their drink with weeping.

They do their civil works with grief. This makes them labor with sorrow in their particular callings. It was Solomon's trouble to think that a fool should have the rule of his labor wherein he labored, and showed himself wise under the sun (Ecclesiastes 2:18–20). And the sad case is often observed that the same estates which were the fruit of the wise and good parents' prayers and diligence are consumed upon the children's lusts, and that the good creatures which were a blessing to the parents, and wherewith they honored God and fed Christ in his members, prove to be a curse to their children, and weapons in their hand wherewith they fight against God and His people.

This also causes them to do their religious works in grief and sorrow. I shall only give you two particulars:

This makes them instruct these poor, ungodly children with sorrow. It is a doleful case when men can have their dogs come when they whistle, their horse yield to the bridle, and their oxen to submit to the yoke; but their unruly children will not be subject to the holy government of their parents. They can readily learn filthy words and wicked actions from their ungodly schoolfellows, fellow apprentices, or debauched companions, but they will not hear the instruction of their father, nor obey the law of their mother.

This causes them to pray for such children with sorrow. For according as is the spiritual state of the children, so are their holy parents affected in prayer to God for them. When they can in prayer call upon God as the Father of their children, and can present their children to God as such who are born of God and adopted by Him, and can beg mercy for them who are the vessels of mercy, then they do, as the apostle did for the Philippians (1:4), in every prayer make request for them with joy. But when children are manifestly wicked, their good parents must in prayer to God call them what they are, and must say, "Lord, my poor children are children of the devil, children of disobedience, children of Thy wrath, lying, swearing, covetous, drunken, unclean, stubborn children; oh pity, pardon, save, convert them." They pray for them, but they pray in the sorrow and anguish of their souls.

5. I will now show how wicked children embitter all the comforts of their good parents, so that, as Solomon tells us in Proverbs 17:21, "A father of a fool hath no joy." I shall exemplify this in four particulars.

First, the good parents cannot be so comfortable and delightful to one another as they would be when both are in bitterness for their wicked children. The husband cannot be such a comfort to his wife when he is almost in continual anger and sorrow for his wicked child, nor the wife such a delight to her husband when her heart is bleeding for her ungodly child. For if they have no joy in themselves, as was said before, they cannot be so much the joy and delight of one another. But when they lie down, this makes them water their bed with tears; and they awake with sorrow with a wicked child on their hearts.

Second, they cannot take so much comfort as they would in the other children who are godly—not that they love them less, but rather more. But their joy in them is much interrupted hereby. Suppose among many children there is but one ungodly child, if that one is a disturbance and annoyance to the whole family that one sinner (as Solomon speaks in a more general case) destroys much good. It grieves them to think that whereas that one child was in the same covenant, and had the same dedication to God by baptism, and the same affection and education from the parents with all the other children, yet the rest are vessels of mercy, but this one seems to be a vessel of wrath.

Third, they cannot take so much comfort in the victory over their own sins when they see the same corruptions which are abhorred and mortified and forsaken by the parents, breaking out and reigning in the children.

Fourth, this interrupts their joy in God and Jesus Christ when such parents must with the same faith believe God's wrath to their children as they believe His love to themselves; and when they look upon God as their Father, they must look upon Him as an enemy to their children. And when they say, "We hope heaven is our portion and place," it must grieve them that their children will not go there with them.

6. The greatness of this affliction appears further by the concomitants of it. I shall only instance three things that usually accompany it, which make it more grievous.

First, such children often impoverish their parents. Solomon tells us that a wicked child wastes his father and chases away his mother. Such children do not care if they starve their poor parents as long as they can feed their own lusts; and it is often seen that a plentiful estate is consumed by riotous children.

Second, such children often debauch and corrupt the other children, and make their brethren in nature to be their brethren in iniquity. And often their brothers and sisters are more easily enticed to sin by a wicked brother than drawn to God by a godly father. And if any of the other children are godly, these wicked ones hate and revile and persecute them like wicked Cain, who slew his brother because his works were righteous.

Third, they bring reproach upon that good religion which their good parents profess and practice; and thus Eli's sons made men abhor the offerings of the Lord. With some, the holy lives of the parents cannot wipe off the reproach which is cast on religion by the wickedness of their children.

7. The greatness of this affliction appears by these eight aggravations of it:

First, it aggravates their grief to remember what pleasure and delight these children were to them in their childhood; it torments them now to see their sweet and pleasant smiles turned into scornful and disdainful looks at their parents, and their pretty, broken words turned into oaths and lies, and other rotten speeches; it torments them to think that these who were so forward to clasp their arms around their necks, to kiss them, and to run at their commands, now lift up the heel against them.

Second, it aggravates their sorrow to see themselves so miserably disappointed in their former hopes of these children. "Hope deferred (said Solomon) makes the heart sick," but to be crossed and disappointed in hopes of such great mercy even breaks the heart. When these parents remember how pleasant it was to them to hear these children lisp out their catechisms, and to hear their good words of God and Christ, it cannot but be very grievous to them that the same children whom with Hannah they lent to the Lord should sell themselves to the devil.

Third, it aggravates their sorrow that their children are so void of love to their parents, and to see that the company of liars, drunkards, whoremongers and thieves is more delightful to them than the company of their parents.

Fourth, it aggravates their sorrow to look upon the holy children of others and say, "Yonder are children that make a glad father and mother, when the children of our bodies and counsels and prayers and vows and tears live as if their father was an Amorite and their mother an Hittite!"

Fifth, it aggravates the parents' sorrow when they have but one child, and that one proves to be foolish and disobedient. Of this there are many instances. The Scripture, to set forth the saddest kind of mourning, compares it to mourning for an only son. Jeremiah 6:26: "Make thee mourning as for an only son, most bitter lamentation." Zechariah 12:10: "They shall mourn as one that mourneth for an only son." I know that these Scriptures speak of parents mourning for the death of an only son, but it is not so sad to follow an only son to the grave as to see an only child live to the dishonor of God, to be a curse to his generation, and to be continually destroying his precious son. It is a very bitter case when as much love, kindness, care, cost, pains, prayers, and fastings are bestowed upon one child as other parents bestow upon many children. And, notwithstanding all this, one child still proves to be such a monster of wickedness, as if the sins of many ungodly children met in him.

Sixth, it is an aggravation when God's holy ministers are the fathers of fools, which (I have told you) often happens; and this is a most dreadful case for such who have the keys of the kingdom of heaven, and yet must bind over their own children to the wrath of God. Such know the terrors of the Lord and the torments of hell more than others, and therefore must be more affected to believe that this at present is the portion of their own children.

Seventh, it is an aggravation when such children, whom their parents designed to serve God in the ministry of the gospel, prove to be ungodly. This is a matter of great lamentation, for the parents intend them for the highest office in the church, give them education for that end, and then these children make themselves as salt without savor, which is good for nothing but to be cast out and trodden under foot of men.

Eighth, it is an aggravation when children are a grief to their parents in their old age, and do, as it were, throw dirt upon their hoary heads, which is their crown of glory. It is the command of God in Proverbs 23:22: "Despise not thy mother when she is old." Solomon tells us (Ecclesiastes 12) that the days of old age are evil days; their very age is a troublesome and incurable disease. They are like the grasshopper: every light thing is a burden to them. Therefore it must be more troublesome to them to be tormented with wicked children when the strong men (as divines think) Solomon calls "the legs" bow themselves, and their children, who should be a staff and support to them, break their hearts and cause their gray hairs to go with sorrow to the grave.

Chapter 3

Application

Let such parents praise and honor God whom God has blessed with wise and holy and obedient children. Whether by those words in Psalm 144:12 David means children accomplished with natural or spiritual endowments, or both, I shall not determine; but to apply them to the case in hand, I say it is the great mercy of God to you that when so many children are as noisome weeds, your sons should be as hopeful plants grown up in their youth. And when so many make themselves ugly and deformed with sin, your daughters should be as cornerstones (in which is seen the beauty of the building and the art and skill of the workman), polished after the similitude of a palace. Do not hence conclude that you are better parents than others, or that you have had more care in the education of your children than others, but ascribe all to the free grace of God, who will have mercy upon whom He will have mercy.

Let none presume to censure godly parents for their wicked children. "To him that is afflicted," said Job, "pity should be shown him from his friends." Have they not trouble enough already without you adding to their affliction? They have not hereby forfeited the good thoughts and esteem which you should have of them; and if you judge them for this, you must judge as wise and holy saints of God as ever were in the world.

Though God herein sharply corrects them, yet He will not allow you to sit in judgment and to pass sentence upon them. I say to you, as Job to his friends, hold your peace; let them alone; and leave them to stand or fall to their own Master.

This should fill the hearts of these holy parents with revenge upon sin and Satan, which have so debauched and defiled and destroyed their dear children. If a man should murder your child, a spirit of revenge would rise in you and you would say to such a one, "I will have your life and blood for the life and blood of my child." But sin and Satan have destroyed both the precious soul and body of the child; therefore labor, as for other reasons so for this also, to be revenged of them. Labor to do as David did by the lion and the bear which took a lamb out of his flock. He slew both the lion and the bear and delivered the lamb. So do all you can to rescue your poor lambs out of the jaws of Satan; however, labor to hate sin and Satan more, to promote God's honor and kingdom, and the salvation of souls more. And this is the way to be revenged on sin and Satan for the ruin of your children.

I hence exhort holy and obedient children to acknowledge the grace of God to them, that they are or have been the joy and crown of their parents. It is His distinguishing grace that made you to differ from all wicked children, and perhaps from some who came out of the same womb and sucked the same mother's breasts as you did. Consider four things which are great matter of praise:

1. You are the children of holy parents. Consider that you may comfortably come to God in prayer, and say, "We are the children of Thy servant our father; we

are Thy servants, and the children of Thy handmaid our mother." Bless God for your parents' good counsels and examples, and for a great part of a life of prayers, of which you are daily receiving the benefit. If your parents are dead and in heaven, it may put you into a holy and spiritual frame to think of the graces of God that shone in them.

2. The same graces which dwelt in your good parents are in you. Paul speaks of it as a matter of praise to God that the same faith was in Timothy which dwelt first in his grandmother Lois and his mother Eunice; and the Apostle John rejoiced greatly that he found the children of the elect lady walking in truth.

3. You are freed from those stings of conscience which graceless children shall one day feel for their disobedience to their parents. You may joyfully reflect that you were the joy of your holy parents, and that their lives have been made sweeter and their crosses easier by you, that you are the honor and seal of their holy education, when wicked children are the shame and reproach of their parents.

4. You have a right to that rich and precious promise annexed to the Fifth Commandment, and mentioned in Ephesians 6:2–3. By it you may be assured that it shall go well with you both in this world and in the world to come. I seriously profess that I would rather have a right to that one promise made to obedient children than to the best estate and inheritance under the sun.

Chapter 4

Means To Prevent This Calamity

In prescribing some means to be used by those who may be or are parents to prevent this calamity, I shall direct those parents who groan under this calamity as to how to bear it, and then I shall give a serious exhortation to those children who are the grief and bitterness of their parents.

First, I shall prescribe means to be used to prevent this calamity.

1. Use all holy prudence and care in your choice of a spouse; for if you make yourselves the husbands or wives of fools, you are likely in time to become the fathers or mothers of fools. Before the flood, the members of God's church married with a wicked generation (Genesis 6:2), and they brought forth a wicked posterity; but to have a holy spouse is the way to have a holy seed. And therefore what you would most desire to have for yourselves, that labor to find in the person who is to be one flesh with you. You would have yourself born of God; you would have the image of God and the life of Christ in yourself. Labor that these things are in the person whom you choose for your partner. But never make choice of one for your husband or wife whom you would not choose for your companion.

2. Be faithful and upright with God. Proverbs 20:7: "The just man walketh in his integrity, and his chil-

dren are blessed after him." If you would have grace and mercy for your children, love and please the God of all grace and mercy. Whatever secret sins are in you, kill those sins for your poor children's sake lest the sins you too much harbor in your own hearts break out in your children's lives. Parents may often see their own sins against their heavenly Father in their children's disobedience to them. When your children despise you, remember your lack of honor, fear, and reverence of God. When they vex and trouble you, remember how you have grieved and provoked Him. When they decline your company, remember how your hearts have wandered from God in His ordinances.

3. Bewail and beg pardon from God for your failings heretofore to your parents, for many often reap from their own children what they formerly sowed by their sins against their parents; and their miscarriages to their parents fall upon them in the wickedness of their children. The best may sadly reflect upon their want of due honor and obedience and thankfulness to their parents. You may remember your peevish looks and indecent behavior to them, your grieving them in quarreling with your brothers and sisters, your unjust censuring them for partiality in their love to their children, and judging them to lack love for you when you were lacking in your duty to them. And many who are now godly parents themselves may remember that, by greater sins in their youth, they were the grief and bitterness of their fathers and mothers; and therefore pray mightily to God to pardon you, and not to visit these sins upon you in the disobedience of your children.

4. Pray to God not to visit your sins upon your children. When Manasseh was in heaven, Amon his son

followed the steps of his unconverted estate. And Jehoiakim was carried captive into Babylon for the sins of Manasseh. Pray that your children may not be like you in any thing, wherein you are unlike God, and that their teeth may not be set on edge for the sour grapes that you have eaten.

5. Be deeply affected with the corruption of nature in your children. For as no man will value a Savior for himself who is not convinced of the sin and misery which he must be saved from, so you must be sensible of your children's sins, or else you cannot labor for their salvation. When your sweet babes are born, you rejoice to find that in God's book all their members were written. But you should also be sensible of that body of sin they are born with, and that by nature they are young atheists and infidels, haters of God, blasphemers, whoremongers, liars, thieves, and murderers. For they are naturally inclined to these and all other sins, and are by nature children of the wrath of the infinite God. And being convinced of this, you will find that your chief care of them should be to save them from this dreadful state of sin and misery.

6. Be convinced what a great deal of work lies upon you to endeavor the salvation of your children. Young children always make for a great deal of work; they make work for parents, work for servants, and work for all who are around them. But to save them from sin and hell is the greatest work that belongs to their parents. For this reason, parents have a great deal of work to do in their own hearts. They must know and believe and love and obey the doctrine of salvation themselves so that they may be able and fit to instruct their children therein. For a man cannot train up his child in the way

he should go if he does not know the way himself. Deuteronomy 6:6–7: "These words shall be in thy heart, and thou shalt teach them diligently unto thy children." It is fitly rendered in the margin "thou shalt whet or sharpen them." The Word of God is more keen and sharp when it has first done its work on the parents' hearts, and so comes from their hearts to their children. Parents must exercise their own graces in order to put authority and savor in all that they say and do for the salvation of their children. Grace must work in their prayers; grace must rule their tongues; grace must guide the rod, and grace must shine in their lives.

And then it is a great work which is to be wrought in the children; it is a great work for them who are born of the flesh to be born of the Spirit, a great work to make religion and godliness natural to them, to make the children of the devil to become the children of God Almighty. And parents must constantly labor in the use of means to accomplish this work.

7. Be mighty in prayer for your children; for all the good you desire for them must come from God, and therefore must be begged for by prayer. It is in vain for them to be taught of us unless they are taught by God, "whose words, Lord (said holy Augustine), were they but Thine, which by my faithful mother Thou hast sung in my heart." Pray, and pray in faith and hope. "Thy ears (said Augustine again) were at my mother's heart when she prayed for me." You must pray with tender and melting hearts. The same Augustine tells us that his mother's tears watered the earth when she prayed for him. And you must pray for their salvation. Augustine called this the hinge of his holy mother's prayers for him.

8. Solemnly dedicate them to God by baptism; and then you must heartily consent that God alone is the eternal life and happiness of you and your children, and that Jesus Christ is their (and your) Redeemer to redeem you and them from all sin and misery, and to bring both to God. Consent that the Holy Ghost is their (and your) Sanctifier, that by Him you and they may have a Scripture-right unto, and be made meet and fit for, this happiness.

7. When they are capable of it, instruct them in the covenant which by baptism they were solemnly entered into. To this end you must diligently teach them, and they must know, these six things:

(1) They must know the evil and danger of sin; for till they come to know what sin is, what it is to be saved or damned, and what it is to lose or enjoy God, they will not value or accept of Christ, but will despise the Redeemer of the world as being good for nothing. You must therefore labor to make sin odious and Christ precious to your children, and then they will value Christ and obey you. It was prophesied of John the Baptist that he was to prepare the way of the Lord, and to turn the children to the parents. So let it be your care to make way for Christ in your children's hearts. If you prevail in that, they will be obedient to you.

(2) Inform yourselves and them in the doctrine of God the Father, Son, and Holy Ghost. For this is the doctrine whereunto they are baptized; and by baptism they are solemnly entered into covenant with these sacred persons, against the flesh, Satan and the world. Show them the glory and love of God the Father in choosing, ordaining, fitting, and sending Jesus Christ, and in commanding Him to be a sacrifice for us.

Inform them that God the Father is the fountain of life, for Christ lives by the Father. He is the fountain of authority, for Christ received all power in heaven and earth from Him. He is the fountain of all the Christian religion, for Christ first heard these truths from the Father, and then made them known to us. And He is the fountain of glory, for the Father has exalted Christ; and all glorified saints are the blessed of the Father. Labor by these and all other means that God the Father has the greatest place in your children's hearts. Teach them to know and prize Jesus Christ; without this they cannot be true Christians. Show them all the fullness and glory of the Godhead in Jesus Christ; labor to make them see His glory as the only begotten Son of God, and all that He as Mediator and Redeemer has done in the state of His humiliation, and is doing, and will do in the state of His exaltation, for the salvation of lost sinners. Labor to imprint these great truths upon their hearts:

• That it was the will and law of God the Father that God the Son, in our nature, should be a sacrifice for our sins. This fully appears in Hebrews 10:5: "A body hast Thou prepared (or fitted) Me," meaning "to be a sacrifice." And, said He, "Lo, I come to do Thy will, O God." And Psalm 40:8: "Thy law is within my heart," meaning that will and law of the Father which bound Christ to offer and sacrifice Himself for our sins.

• That Jesus Christ, by His obedience to the death of the cross, perfectly obeyed and fulfilled this law and will of God the Father.

• That all salvation and happiness is by the covenant of grace settled upon all (and only) those who believe and obey the Gospel, only for the sake of this sacrifice and obedience of Jesus Christ. And therefore, said the apostle in Hebrews 10:10, "By the which will we are sanctified through the offering of the body of Christ once for all." That is, by Christ's fulfilling the will of his Father in once sacrificing Himself for sinners, we and all true believers are sanctified, that is, perfectly saved.

You must also acquaint them with the office and work of the Holy Ghost, which our Savior tells us in John 16:13 is to guide or lead them into all truth, that is, to enable them to believe and love and obey the saving truths of God revealed in the Gospel. For to the end that they may know and keep their baptismal covenant, they must know how all the three sacred persons, the Father, Son and Holy Ghost, are interested in the great work of salvation.

(3) Labor to convince your children of the excellency of the life of religion and obedience to God. Commend this to them as the most honorable life, for our Savior tell us in John 12:26: "If any man serve Me, him will My Father honor." What shall be done to the man (said Ahasuerus) whom the king will honor? But who is able to tell what shall be done to the man whom the Father of our Lord Jesus Christ will honor? Let them also know that this is the wisest life; it is Job's inquiry, "Where shall wisdom be found?" And Job 28:28: "Behold, the fear of the Lord, that is wisdom; and to depart from evil, is understanding."

Teach them further that it is the safest life, for God is a shield, a rock, and a wall to all who obey Him. And although such things which they have in common with other men are exposed to danger and loss, yet their persons, and their whole portion is always safe. Teach them also that this is the most gainful life, for hereby saints gain God, Christ, and heaven, and lose nothing; for we cannot lose by a Savior who saves us from all evil and brings us into the possession of all good. And though death itself strips us naked of all things under the sun, yet death is an unspeakable gain to all who live this life. And you must further assure them that this is the most pleasant life, for it is a life of faith, love, praise, and joy, and a life of victory over sin. And they who live this life have all things to please them: they have God to please them, Christ and His merits to please them, and a prospect of a holy and blessed eternity to please them. You would never be the fathers and mothers of fools if you could persuade your children to be so wise as to prize and love a life of obedience to God.

(4) Commend to your children the glory and amiableness of the house and Church of God; this is the body whereunto they are baptized. Take your child with you, and go walk about Zion. Go round about her, tell the towers thereof, mark well her bulwarks, and consider her palaces, as you are taught in Psalm 48:12–13. Present to their view King Jesus, and at His right hand standing the Queen (His Church) in gold of Ophir (Psalm 45:9). Say to them, as the angel said to John in Revelation 21:9, "Come hither, and I will show you the bride, the Lamb's wife." Show them that glorious sight in Revelation 12:1, the woman clothed with the sun, and upon her head (that bright and glorious constellation) a crown of twelve stars, so that the company of those who live in communion with God and Jesus Christ may be desirable and delightful to them, and that they may forsake evil company, which is

often the bane of youth.

(5) Teach them to esteem God's ordinances rightly; for by baptism they are solemnly admitted into that house and family which is blessed with these as the means of salvation. Labor to beget in them good thoughts of God's ministers; for you shall ever find that those children will despise you if you make light of them (ministers). Teach them to pray; you can never have comfort in your children till they cry to God, "Abba, Father." Teach them to know and prize and long for the Lord's Supper, and therein to take Christ and all salvation in a little bread and wine. Teach them to honor and delight in the Lord's Day as the diamond in the ring of time. Those children are always the honor and joy of their godly parents who make conscience to keep holy the Lord's Day.

(6) Make them sensible that time is short and precious, that an eternity of glory and misery is at hand, and that death and judgment and heaven or hell are at the door of young children.

9. Labor to save your children from those sins which provoke God and will destroy them, as well as from those sins which will also bring loss and reproach upon you. Some are sadly affected to see their children given to drunkenness, whoredom, or similar sins. But they are not so much concerned for their unbelief, impenitency, want of love to God, and for their covetousness, which shows such parents to have too much of the love of the world and too little love to God and their children's souls. We must take our measures of the evil and danger of sin from the Word of God, which tells us in 1 Corinthians 6:9–10 that the covetous, as well as drunkards and whoremongers, shall not inherit the

kingdom of God. And this will teach parents not only to mourn over a debauched child, but also over a covetous one, though he is a wealthy child.

10. Observe what sins your children are most prone unto, and labor to fill them with revenge and hatred against those sins. If your child had a foot or hand that was gangrened, you would cut off the incurable member rather than bury your child. In the same way you should do what you can to pull out the right eye and to cut off the right hand and the right foot of sin in your children rather than suffer their bodies and souls to be cast into hell. As you should especially kill those sins in yourselves which your natures are most inclined unto, so you should do for your children who are so great a part of yourselves. We are taught in Proverbs 20:11 that even a child is known by his doing, whether his work is pure, or whether it be right. Parents may much discern by the manners and ways of their children in their childhood what they are likely to prove to be in their riper years. And therefore they must observe them so that they may encourage them in the good and discourage them in the evil, which they then appear to be most bent unto.

11. Place your children in families of holiness and prayer if they must leave home. You will not plant your trees among briars and thorns, much less should you choose to place your children to serve those who will not serve God.

12. Give them due correction. God has commanded this to kill their sins and to save their souls. Proverbs 23:13–14: "Withhold not correction from the child; for if thou beatest him with the rod, he shall not die. Thou shalt beat him with the rod, and shalt deliver his soul

from hell." It is better that your child is whipped than damned; and do not let your child's weeping and crying under the rod move you to withhold due correction. Proverbs 19:18: "Chasten thy son, and let not thy soul spare for his crying." If your child's bone be out of joint, you will have it set, though he cries and bawls under the hand of the surgeon. You would say instead, "It is better that he cries now than be lame as long as he lives." So it is better that your children cry now under the rod of their father than that they should weep and wail forever under the wrath of the infinite God.

And therefore, that you may perform this duty, take these six directions:

DIRECTION 1. Do not allow your servants to correct your children; for correction is an act of authority, and therefore cannot belong to those who are merely your servants. I would not have parents to permit their children to despise and abuse their servants, but for parents to allow their servants to correct their children is the way to make their children stubborn, their servants proud, and the parents themselves contemptible in the eyes of both.

DIRECTION 2. Convince them that it is your duty to correct them for their sins; and therefore it is advisable that you make them memorize those Scriptures which bind you to correct them. Also make them memorize those Scriptures which condemn the sins which you correct them for, so that their consciences may justify you in doing your duty, and that they may be more afraid of sin than the rod, and more afraid of provoking God than offending you.

DIRECTION 3. Correct them quickly (Proverbs 13:24). And Proverbs 19:18: "Chasten thy son while there is hope." Use the rod wisely on them before they become scourges and scorpions to you.

DIRECTION 4. Labor to be in a good frame when you correct them, that love, prudence, and meekness, and not rage and fury, may govern the rod. And do not exercise too much severity towards them so that you may not provoke them to wrath, lest the wrath of the children proves to be the grief of the parents.

DIRECTION 5. Pray to God for a blessing upon your correcting them so that it may be effectual to drive out that foolishness which is bound up in their hearts.

DIRECTION 6. Be good examples to your children. Let them not see you in any sin, for that may infect them and make them despise you; but let them always see you shining in the image of God, and that is the way to make them honor and obey you in the Lord. Live so that you may say to them, as Paul to the Philippians (4:9), "Those things which ye have both learned, and received, and heard, and seen in me [us], do, and the God of love and peace shall be with you."

Chapter 5

Directions For Bearing This Calamity

I proceed now to direct those parents who are under this calamity how to bear it.

DIRECTION 1. Abhor it as a great sin to faint under this affliction, that is, either to be disabled for your duty or to sink in your comforts. For it is a sign that you placed too much of your happiness in your children if their wickedness makes you faint under this calamity. I shall only plead with you as Joab did with David, when he made that bitter lamentation for his son Absalom in 2 Samuel 19:6: "Thou hast declared this day that thou regardest neither princes, nor servants." So I say to you, you hereby declare that you do not regard God and Christ if your soul faints under the burden of a disobedient child.

DIRECTION 2. Consider what I have proved, that this is an affliction which ordinarily befalls God's dearest children. You must not think of this as if you were the first godly parents of ungodly children, or as if herein some strange thing happened unto you. I confess where a calamity seems singular or extraordinary, it is more apt to overwhelm the afflicted because they will be then apt to think that there is some extraordinary displeasure in God against them, and to say with the Church, "Behold and see if there be any sorrow like unto my sorrow, wherewith the Lord hath afflicted me in the day of His fierce anger" (Lamentations 1:12). But this affliction is ordinary, and is consistent with the saving and distinguishing grace of God to them; and is a rod that is usually lain on the lot of the righteous.

DIRECTION 3. Consider that there might have befallen you greater miseries than this. I will give you three greater evils which would have made you more miserable.

First, you might have been a wicked, ungodly wretch yourself. And for the great Jehovah to have cursed and damned you forever would have made you unspeakably more miserable than to be tormented a while with a wicked child.

Second, you might have had an ungodly spouse to be as rottenness in your bones. Solomon seems to speak of a troublesome spouse as being more grievous than a wicked child. Proverbs 19:13: "A foolish son is the calamity of his father, and the contentions of a wife are a continual dropping." This is like the constant dropping of rain into a house, which rots the building, spoils the goods, and ruins both house and inhabitants; and to the extent that your spouse is nearer, and ought to be dearer to you than your child, to be afflicted therein is a greater calamity.

Third, God might have left all your children to perish in their sins; but if you have even one godly child, your joy in that should greatly abate your sorrow for your other wicked children.

DIRECTION 4. Consider that you have greater things to affect you with grief and sorrow than your wicked children; there are whole empires and kingdoms of men and women and children who have as precious souls as yours or your children's. These dishonor the same God and perish under His wrath, and multitudes who have the Scriptures and ordinances despise the same Christ and the same gospel as your children do. And why should you be more concerned for one or more of your wicked children than for the whole world that lies in wickedness?

DIRECTION 5. Let your sorrow be guided by Scripture and reason, so that you may not provoke God, defile your souls, and wound your consciences by sinful groans and tears. For this end observe two rules:

First, mourn more for their sins whereby they provoke and dishonor God, and defile and destroy themselves and others, than for any shame or loss in worldly things that befall you hereby. In this way it may appear that the love of God and your children's souls, and not the love of the world, has the greatest influence on your sorrow. For I fear that there is usually in good parents too much of carnal sorrow and too little of godly sorrow in their mourning under this great calamity.

Second, do not let your sorrow disease your body and impair your health. God does not require us to mourn more for our children's sins than our own, and He never makes it our duty by sorrow for either to destroy our bodies, which are the temples of the Holy Ghost. The truth is that godly sorrow is the health of the soul and never hurts the body. For grace is always a friend and never an enemy to nature. And therefore do not deprive yourself of all opportunities to honor God and serve His Church. Do not make your spouse desolate, nor your children orphans, by such sorrow that will neither please God, ease yourself, nor do any good to your wicked and miserable children.

DIRECTION 6. Labor to get your graces strengthened under this great affliction; for you have need of more knowledge, wisdom, faith, hope, love, meekness, and patience to enable and fit you to bear this than most other affections. And you must see and enjoy more of God and Christ to keep your hearts up under this than under most other troubles. Yet by the strength of Christ you may be enabled not only to bear this tribulation, but to glory in it. And the greater the trouble is, the more good you may gain by it.

DIRECTION 7. Comfort yourself in that the greatest and best things which you have most prayed for, trusted unto, expected, and chiefly loved and desired, are all safe and sure.

God is and will be blessed and glorious forever, whatever becomes of your child. All His infinite perfections are working for His glory. Christ Himself is God's, and does the whole work of a Mediator as His servant and for His glory. All the blessed angels and saints will forever honor, admire, love, and praise Him.

God the Father, Son, and Holy Ghost are forever your own, and will to all eternity be glorified in making you blessed and glorious. You have a bad child, but a good God; all your work will be done, your sins pardoned and killed, your graces perfected, and your body and soul glorified—and shall an ungodly child make all your consolations herein small to you?

DIRECTION 8. Last, consider this trouble will last but a little while. I confess I do not know, or can upon search find, anything that can lift up the heart above this trouble but the knowledge and sense of the infinite love of God in Christ to a man's self, and of that holy and glorious eternity which this love will shortly bring him unto. To tell you that this is and has been the case of other godly parents may allay something of your grief. But what is this but to tell you that others are and have been as miserable as you, or to tell you that children as wicked as yours have been sanctified and saved yields some hopes? But it can amount to nothing more than to think that they may be saved or they may be damned, and there is as much reason to fear the one as to hope for the other. But for a man to see a gainful death, ready to loose him into that world where there is none of this sorrow, and to know that at the day of judgment his wicked children will be no more to him than bloody Bonners [a heretic], Gardiners [a traitor], or damned devils, and that he himself shall sit with Christ to judge them; and that he shall love and delight in the holiness and justice of the Judge of all the world in passing that sentence upon them, "Depart ye cursed into everlasting fire, prepared for the devil and his angels"—this is sufficient to overcome all immoderate grief for his ungodly children.

Chapter 6

A Serious Exhortation to Ungodly Children

I shall begin to close this discourse with a serious exhortation to those ungodly children who are the grief and bitterness of their good parents. And herein I shall (1) endeavor to convince them of their sins, (2) convince them of their misery, and (3) persuade them to forsake their sins so that they may be freed from that misery.

1. I shall set before you the greatness of your sins in these four particulars:

You have broken your covenant with God.

You have broken the bonds wherein you were bound to the church of God.

You have broken the bonds of your duty to your parents.

You have broken the bonds of your duty to your other relations.

First, you have broken your covenant with God, whereunto you were solemnly entered by baptism; for it is clear from Leviticus 19:3 that by casting off the authority of your parents, you have disowned the Lord to be your God. Your breach of covenant with God appears more fully in the following particulars:

• In your hearts and practices, you deny the being of God. The first article of the covenant is that you should acknowledge and believe that the Lord is God; for "he that cometh to God must believe that He is" (Hebrews

11:6). But this is the language of your hearts and lives: "There is no God." You deny God to be the first and best Being by preferring the creatures before Him, and saying, in effect, that the creatures are all, and the great Jehovah is but as a cipher to you.

• You deny His omnipresence. He fills all places where you are, but you take no notice of Him. The presence of a father or master has some influence upon you, but it does not at all work upon you that God is in the room.

• You deny His infinite wisdom, that wisdom God shows in contriving the work of salvation by Jesus Christ. I say, that wisdom which is so glorious and wonderful to the principalities and powers of heaven is to such proud and ignorant boys and girls as you but a foolish and ridiculous thing.

• You deny His power in daring to war against Him. And like those warrior-like atheists spoken of in Job 15:25–26, you stretch out your hands against God, and strengthen yourselves against the Almighty; you run at Him, even grab His neck, as if you were able to fight God and overcome the Almighty.

• You deny His holiness, and think that God is altogether such a one as yourselves (Psalm 50:21). So that you may not be terrified by your enmity and unlikeness to Him, you will please yourselves in fancying that God is like you; as if you must rather be a pattern to Him than He be a pattern to you. And so you will persuade yourselves that He is the God of atheists, whoremongers, drunkards, liars, and thieves, and not the holy God of a holy people.

• You deny the truth of God. One of the greatest and best truths that ever God spoke to man is that found in

1 John 5:11: "God hath given to us eternal life, and this life is in His Son." And yet herein you would make him a liar by not believing this solemn record which He gave of Christ. A liar is one of the worst characteristics of the devil, and this you give to the true and holy God. These things I write, as it were, upon the brazen faces of all ungodly and disobedient children.

You break the covenant, in refusing to take God for your God and happiness; the greatest promise that ever God made to man is that Hebrews 8:10, I will be to you a God. But this signifies nothing to you; you will not accept of him for your chief honor and treasure and joy. It is no honor to you to have the great Jehovah for your Father. You see no good in him, and account not yourselves the better for him. And if you lose him, you think you lose nothing. You neither love, nor desire him, nor take any delight or pleasure in him.

• You have broken the covenant by renouncing God the Father, Son and Holy Ghost, in whose name you were baptized. Your lives declare that you would rather have the love of a debauched companion than the love of the Father of Jesus Christ. You despise the Lord Jesus, account the great price of redemption to be worth nothing, and would rather keep your sins than be saved from them. You defy the wrath of God, and scorn that the Mediator should make your peace with Him. You resist the Holy Spirit, and would rather be made filthy and wicked, and be taught to lie, swear, and steal than that the Spirit should teach you to love, serve, and delight in God.

• You have broken the covenant by taking part with the devil, the world, and sin, against the Father, Son and Holy Ghost. You have done this by believing the promises of the devil, the world and sin, and by not believing the promises of God. The devil, the world and sin are the three great cheats of mankind, and they deceive men by making seemingly great and high promises. And by these they have prevailed with man to break both the covenant of works and the covenant of grace. The devil tempted our first parents not to believe that word of God which He gave them to deter and keep them from sin, which word is written in Genesis 2:17: "In the day thou eatest thereof thou shalt surely die." The devil tempted them to look on that word as a lie, and makes them a great promise (Genesis 3:4–5) that if they eat the forbidden fruit, they shall not only be safe from all evil, saying, "Ye shall not surely die," but that they shall also be preferred to greater happiness than God had then placed them in. For, said he, "your eyes shall be opened, and ye shall be as gods, knowing good and evil." And by believing this promise of the devil, they broke the covenant of life and brought that deluge of sin and misery which came upon all mankind. And since he prevailed with men not to believe the word of God which He spoke to keep them from sin and destruction, now his work is to tempt them to make God a liar in the word which He has spoken to save them from sin and ruin by Jesus Christ. And this is the word of the covenant of grace, which promises eternal life and salvation to all who believe in Christ, repent of their sins, and live the lives of new creatures, according to the rules of the gospel. But the devil tempts men to break this covenant by promising them life and all happiness in a course of sin. And these wicked children believe the devil herein, and bless themselves in their sins, saying with those bold ranters in Deuteronomy 29:19, "We shall have peace, though we walk in the imagination of our own hearts to add drunkenness to thirst." And thus you break your covenant with God, and make a covenant with death and hell.

In obeying the devil, the world, and sin, and in disobeying God, you call God your Father in heaven, but you do the lusts of the devil, your father in hell. You walk according to the course of this world (Ephesians 2:2) and are the servants of sin (Romans 6:20). You hate and fight against God, your Maker and Redeemer. Were it possible for you, you would every day kill Him who alone has immortality. And thus, like a company of renegades, you live as if you were baptized in the name of the devil, the world and the flesh, and renounce the Father, Son and Holy Ghost.

Second, you have broken the bonds of your duty to the Church of God. You were born members of the Church, and subjects of the kingdom of Jesus Christ; by baptism were solemnly admitted into that great and holy and victorious and blessed society. Hebrews 12:22–23: "Mt. Zion, the city of the living God, the heavenly Jerusalem, the general assembly and church of the first-born written in heaven." But you have forsaken this Church and turned yourselves out of the family and house of the living God, and have become of the same party with the devil and his seed; you have labored to fill the world with sin and the kingdom of Satan. And you would have Jesus Christ to have no name, kingdom, ministers, ordinances, or people in the world.

Third, you have broken the bonds of your duty to your parents. This appears in that those black characteristics already given of wicked children are found in you; whereunto I shall add this one, which includes all the particulars of your disobedience which can be mentioned, namely, you do not love your parents. For love works no evil unto, but always wills and seeks the good of the beloved. Love ever inclines persons to please them whom they love, and to love and delight in their company; it causes such looks, words, and behaviors as are expressions of love. How pleasant has it been sometimes to me to see, as it were, the heart and soul of a child running out in his pleasant and loving looks to his parents! But you disobedient children do not love your parents, but rather do them harm, and cause them more sorrow than all the malicious enemies and persecutors they ever met with in the world. You are always vexing, crossing, and provoking them, and are as continual pricks in their eyes, thorns in their sides, and would rather be with liars, swearers, and drunkards, and with your wanton and idle companions, than with your wise, grave, and holy parents. How merry and jovial are you in the company of such who will join with you to serve the devil, dishonor God, and destroy your souls! But how uneasy, lumpish, sour, and discontent are you in the presence of your parents! Your spiteful looks, sullen words, and scornful carriage betray your hatred, anger, and envy against your good parents. Ah, wicked wretches, that you cannot find in your hearts to love your parents, from whom you had your beings under God, and who have used all holy means to make you holy and blessed.

Fourth, you have broken the bonds of your duty to your other relations and to all men. You cannot be good brothers or sisters while you are such bloody children to your parents. You cannot be good servants or apprentices, or good husbands or wives, or good subjects to magistrates, while you are bad children. For the same sins that debauch you in that relation will debauch you in all, and will make you an encumbrance to your place, the troublers of the world, and a very plague and curse to your generation.

2. I shall now endeavor to convince you of your misery. And, oh, that I had a heart and tongue to think and speak of this as the matter requires! Consider that you are cursed children. Deuteronomy 27:16: "Cursed be he that setteth light by his father or his mother, and all the people shall say, 'Amen.' " Observe that God Himself here proclaims you to be cursed. He alone can curse or bless you, having all curses and blessings at His command. He can set His love or pour out His wrath where He pleases. He is able and faithful to fulfill his own threatenings, and He knows you to be cursed, for He knows all the children of His grace and all the children of His wrath. Observe further that all God's ministers are to pronounce you cursed, according to verse 14: "The Levites shall speak, and say to all the men of Israel with a loud voice, 'Cursed be he that setteth light by his father or his mother.' " The ministers of God must with a loud voice, as if they would ring in the ears of all, declare you to be cursed. And I, a minister of the gospel, do hereby proclaim all wicked and disobedient children (though some of them may be the fruit of my own body) to be cursed. Nay further, all people, yea your own selves are to judge you cursed; and all the people shall say, "Amen." They and you are to believe it, and to approve of it as most just and righteous, that you are cursed.

But that I may convince you of your misery, I shall further set before you these four things:

First, you are out of the way of all good. God has His way of mercy and His way of wrath. And you are out of the way of His mercy, for you do not stand in the grace and love of God which causes all good. You are children of His wrath, which causes all misery. And (as I have told you) you have broken that covenant which conveys all grace and mercy, so that no good can come to you unless you turn to God and your parents.

Second, you are on the very way and road to all wickedness. Many of the most horrid sins in the world first began in disobedience to parents. And most of those who have turned out to be liars, drunkards, whoremongers, thieves, and murderers were first ungodly and disobedient children.

Third, you are in continual danger of some remarkable judgment of God in this life. Exodus 21:17: "He that curseth (or revileth) his father or his mother shall surely be put to death." Proverbs 20:20: "Whoso curseth his father or his mother, his lamp shall be put out in obscure darkness." Your lamp of life and pleasure may seem to burn and shine at the present, but there is a black and dismal night hastening on all disobedient children. Proverbs 30:17: "The eye that mocketh his father, and despiseth to obey his mother, the ravens of the valley shall pick it out, and the young eagles shall eat it." None are more likely to pass into the eternal world through a shameful and untimely death than disobedient children. When God leaves children to disobey their parents, it is a dreadful sign of their approaching ruin. It is recorded of Eli's sons in 1 Samuel 2:25 that "they hearkened not unto the voice of their father, because the Lord would slay them."

Fourth, if you go on in your course of disobedience,

you will forever be damned in hell; for (I say) you have broken that covenant which promises eternal life to all who believe and obey the Gospel, and just as certainly binds over to the wrath and vengeance of God all who live in disobedience to God and their parents. Miserable children! I have sent this poor little book to overtake you before the wrath and vengeance of God overtake you. I am not altogether a stranger to the terrors of the Lord. I know what is before you, and what a meeting there will quickly be between God and you better than you do. I have labored to affect my heart in seeing what lies at your door. I know that while you are following the chase of your filthy pleasures, evil from God is hunting you and will find you out to destroy you. And I dare not damn my own soul by not warning you of those sins which will be the damnation of yours. Foolish boys and girls can now laugh at hearing of death and hell and judgment to come; and when ministers sound the trumpet in their ears, and give them warning of these things, foolish children can, like the warhorse in Job, say among the trumpets, "Aha," for the devil tempts his children to make sport of those things at which he trembles himself. But when I remember how I have seen in some of you your down-looks, your pale faces, your shivering limbs; and as Job speaks of the adulterer when he comes to be known (Job 24:17), that you have been as in the terrors of the shadow of death when your mortal parents have found you out in your sins, I cannot but think how your countenances will fall and your stout spirits sink and your mettle fail when ye come to fall into the hands of the living God.

3. I come now to exhort and persuade you to abhor and forsake your sins so that you may escape this mis-

ery. I would have you to repent and believe with the saints of God so that you may be saved before you come to repent with the damned in hell, and with the devils to believe and tremble. For this end I shall endeavor to convince you of your folly, and then in the last chapter direct you how to attain true wisdom.

First, I shall endeavor to convince you of your folly. You see the text calls a wicked son a foolish son. God, who knows you best, and has a true judgment of you, calls you fools, and would have all the world to be of the same judgment with Himself, and therefore to account you as fools. And you will at last call yourselves fools when ye come to have the portion of fools. And unless you judge yourselves to be fools, you cannot be wise.

And that ye may, as in a glass, see your own folly, I shall propound to you these five questions. As God said to Job, so do I in His name say to you, "Gird up your loins like men. I will demand of you, and answer me" (Job 38:3).

QUESTION 1. Are you not very fools in that in your hearts and lives you deny the being of God? There are no worse fools than they who say in their hearts, "There is no God" (Psalm 14:1)? For such a one says in effect that there is no religion, no sin, no heaven, and no hell; yea, he says that he himself is nothing, and that there are neither heavens, nor earth, nor seas, nor men, nor beasts, nor any other creatures. For if there is no God, there can be nothing else; so that you have the name of fools written on your foreheads. And as it is said in Ecclesiastes 10:3, you say to every man that you are a company of fools.

QUESTION 2. Are you not fools to make such a foolish choice? It is the infinite goodness of God that you have life and death, blessing and cursing set before you; and that you have God, Christ, the Holy Spirit, and the heavenly glory to choose. And you have beings capable of choosing them; you may take them for your own and use them as your own every day; you are called and commanded to choose them, and have time and opportunity to choose them, and shall certainly have them if you choose them. And yet these, as Solomon says in Proverbs 17:16, are but as a price in the hands of a fool who has no heart for it.

Consider that there are two sorts of affections in all human creatures, and all are wise or fools, according as they set and place these. There are affections of union, such as love, desire and delight, which unite the heart to their objects. And there are affections of opposition, such as hatred and anger, which separate the heart from their objects. And are you not monstrous fools in that you hate and abhor God and your Redeemer, in whom there are all reasons for your love and desires and joy, and in that you love, desire, and delight in sin, the devil, death, and hell, in whom there are all reasons for the hatred and revenge of your souls? To love those things which are altogether loathsome, and to hate what is altogether lovely, is a plain argument of your madness and folly.

QUESTION 3. Are you not fools in allowing everything to deceive you? The Scripture tells you that the devil is a deceiver; it tells you of the deceitfulness of your hearts, of the deceitfulness of sin, of the deceitfulness of riches, of the deceitfulness of wine and strong drink, of the deceitfulness of harlots (who promise pleasure, but prove to be a deep ditch and a narrow pit), of the deceitfulness of a lying tongue (which promises that lies shall serve the liar's turn and do his work, but proves to be but for a moment), of the deceitfulness of theft and unjust gain, which seems sweet at present, but soon afterwards proves as gravel in the mouth. And yet, notwithstanding all the shame, rags, stings, and torments of conscience which have come upon you by trusting in these, you will still believe them, and allow yourselves by these deceivers to be cheated of God and Christ, of your souls and your time, and of heaven.

QUESTION 4. Are you not fools in being so set and bent to ruin and destroy yourselves? Proverbs 18:7: "A fool's mouth is his own destruction, and his lips are the snare of his soul." Ecclesiastes 10:12: "The lips of a fool shall swallow up himself." You are so bent on your own ruin that your hearts rise in anger and hatred against your good parents and ministers, and all who labor to save you. You account them to be your worst enemies who would not have you damned! Miserable children, allow yourselves but one hour's serious consideration of your eternal estate and you will see reasons to condemn yourselves as a company of proud and ignorant fools in attempting to run down God and His kingdom and religion, and in valuing your draughts and lusts and lies at such a rate as to exchange them for the eternal life and happiness of your souls.

QUESTION 5. Are you not fools in not preparing for death and judgment, which are ready to overtake you? To convince you of this, be informed that men are prepared for death and judgment who by faith, repentance, and holiness have become heirs of the promises of the gospel, and so have a right unto and fitness for all that glory which, in performance of these promises, God will give them the possession at those great days.

But men are unprepared when they are under the wrath and curse of God, and are condemned to those eternal torments which are threatened in the Scriptures, and will at death and judgment be executed upon them.

Now examine yourselves by these things, and you may then see what fools you are in not preparing for these days. For if you were prepared, you would then enter into a world where all will love you. God, Christ, all the angels, and all the saints will love you; and you will forever be holy and blessed in their love to you and in your love to them. But being unprepared, you must then be cast into a world where all will hate you, and where you will hate all the holy and blessed. God will there hate you, and be a consuming fire against you. The devils and all the damned in hell will hate you, and you will hate them.

And we find that our Savior branded him as a fool (Luke 12:20) who promised himself an easy and merry life for many years, when that very night he was to lose his soul. And He gives the character of "foolish virgins" (Matthew 25:2) to those who were unprepared for that great and terrible and sudden cry, "The bridegroom is come, go ye out to meet him." Poor children! Let these common things be imprinted on your hearts. Death is certain; the day of death is as certainly appointed as was the day of your birth. And as your birth kept its time, so will your death keep its time. You cannot sin away death, though you sin away the sense of it. Consider also that death is near. Whatever you think of your lives, they will be but as a vapor, a shadow, or smoke, as God speaks them to be. And though you put death far from you, yet it will be within a hand's breadth of you. One day or hour may put an end to your space of repentance, conclude your day of grace and salvation, and dispatch you into that world where no new creatures are made. You now defy death, as if you were a fit match for the king of terrors. You scorn the grave, scoff at the day of judgment, and deride everlasting burnings. But when God shall pour upon you your own wickedness (Jeremiah 14:16), then you will too late condemn yourselves as fools when you come to reap the fruit of your own folly.

Chapter 7

Directions to True Wisdom

I come now to give you directions to true wisdom, so that you may be such wise children as to make your fathers glad, and not be the heaviness of your mothers.

1. Do not dare to put off your repentance any longer. It is not too late to repent, so long as God calls you to repentance and gives you time for it. Yet is the accepted time, it is the day of salvation. God, Christ, angels, the church, and your bleeding parents are yet ready to receive you in love and joy. But it will shortly be too late to repent, though it can never be too soon. Dear children! You must either persuade yourselves that the Word of God is a lie, and so think ye are secure from hell because you deny the Bible that threateneth it, or you must presume that you are not ungodly children, as indeed you are. If you will not be so persuaded, then you must conclude that your present state is not safe and good, and that therefore you must either repent or be damned. Perhaps the devil does not tempt you to resolve that you will never repent, but rather to think that there is yet time enough, and that therefore you will repent hereafter.

I have sometimes dreaded to hear debauched children confidently say that they do not question but they shall be converted and become good, when at present they hate to be reformed. Yea, I am persuaded that some secure themselves in their sins by presuming that the prayers of their good parents for their conversion and salvation will at last be heard. But how many such have been (as Solomon speaks of others in Proverbs 14:32) driven away in their wickedness; in whom that dreadful Scripture hath been fulfilled: "He that being often reproved, hardeneth his neck, shall suddenly be destroyed, and that without remedy" (Proverbs 29:1).

I shall here seriously reason this case a little with you. Why would you continue one moment longer in those sins which you must repent of or perish? Why would you defer repentance, for which you shall have cause forever to rejoice and bless God when it is done? Are you not wicked enough already? Will you wait to become worse? Have you not defiled yourselves, provoked God, refused Christ, and afflicted your parents long enough already? Poor souls! If there is one hour yet left wherein you are sure that you shall not die and fall into hell; or one hour wherein sin is better than grace, and wherein it is better to be a child of the devil than a child of God; or if you can come into the kingdom of God and begin an eternal life an hour too soon, take that hour and spend it on your lusts. But if not, stop immediately, and let this be the hour wherein you begin to believe and repent and reform, and wherein you begin to set your faces towards heaven with an unmovable resolution to walk in the way of faith and obedience till you come there.

2. Judge whether you have more reason to obey the devil or to obey God. The apostles asked their persecutors in Acts 4:19 whether it was right in the sight of God to hearken to them more than unto God. So I ask you whether it is right to obey the devil rather than God, you just judge. Consider, God has authority to com-

mand you, for He is your Maker, your Preserver, and your Redeemer, and you owe yourselves to Him. But the devil neither made, nor kept, nor bought you, and therefore can have no right to command you.

Consider further that all the commands of God are the commands of His love; for he not only commands you as your Lord, but also as your Father and Savior. And therefore He commands you to take Him to be your God and happiness, to take His Son Jesus Christ to save you from all evil and to make you forever holy and blessed. But the devil commands you out of hatred and malice, and all his commands are the commands of a murderer. Therefore he commands you to defile, to destroy, and to damn yourselves. He commands you to be blind and ignorant, to hate and scorn God and Christ, and to love sin, death and hell.

Consider also that God is able to reward your obedience and to punish your disobedience. He is the only Lawgiver who is able to both save and destroy (James 4:12). He can crown you with eternal glory if you obey Him, and He can cast you into everlasting flames if you disobey Him. But the devil, who is cursed and tormented himself, cannot make you happy if you obey him, nor can he make you miserable if you forsake and renounce him.

3. See the great difference between those wise and holy children who live in obedience to God and their parents, and you who live in disobedience to both. It is not wealth or poverty, beauty or or deformity, or sickness or health, but sin and grace that make the greatest difference between persons. And you must know God and Christ, or else you cannot understand the worth of a saint nor the vileness of a sinner. Some of you may

look into your own families and there see some of your brethren and sisters like pleasant and fruitful plants about your father's table, while you are as briars, thorns, and weeds in the family. They are the crown and joy, and you are the calamity of your parents. All who see them may look upon them as a seed whom the Lord has blessed, but all who see you have reason to judge you to be a cursed generation. Poor children! Is it better to be like Cain than like Abel, like cursed Canaan than like Shem, like Ishmael than like Isaac, or like Esau than like Jacob? Are not your souls and bodies as precious as the souls and bodies of your good brethren and sisters? Can the devil, sin, and the world be better to you than to them? Is not death and judgment as near you as it is to them? Have you not as much reason to love and obey God and your parents as they? Can you endure the loss of heaven or the torments of hell better than they? If not, why would you not be as good as they are?

4. Do nothing but what you are willing should be known; if you would not have your parents, your masters, your magistrates, and your friends and foes know your lies, lusts, thefts, profaning the Lord's Day, and your haunting evil company, do not practice these things. You need not fear who knows how holy, just, sober, and chaste you are. Religion can boldly show its shining face to God and man; but sin makes you sneaky, cowardly, base and fearful; it imprints marks of dishonor and shame upon your looks and countenances, and fills you with horror and consternation when you are discovered. Consider seriously that all from whom your greatest shame and misery will come know you. The devils know you, and will accuse,

disgrace, and torment you for the same sins they tempted you to. And they will not help you to hide your sins when time of grace and repentance and pardon is past. Your own hearts and consciences know you, and will awaken out of their present sleep to condemn and sting you. And God, who is greater than all, knows you. All your secret sins are in the light of His countenance, and He will bring them all to judgment. And it will then fully appear to angels and devils, and to saints and sinners, what you are.

5. Therefore, do not be such now as you dare not, at the hour of death, profess yourselves to be. Religion and godliness is at all times to be professed before God and angels and men. Romans 10:10: "For with the heart man believeth, and with the mouth confession is made to salvation." But what monsters would you appear to yourselves if you professed yourselves to be what you are? Suppose you were reading this but one hour before you die, and must say, "We are now falling into the hands of the living God. And by the time that the glass run out and the clock strikes next, we are to give account of ourselves to the Judge of all the world." Would you dare then to say, "We profess ourselves to be haters of God, children of the devil, and despisers of our holy parents, and we choose the way to hell"?

6. Consider what account you can give in being such burdens on the earth, and in being so grievous and chargeable to all who are concerned with you. Is it nothing to you to be as biles or scabs on the body, or a stinking smell, or an infectious disease in the house and family where you are, or as weeds in a garden, to cumber and annoy your place? You will pay dearly one day for all the sighs, groans and tears which you have

caused your afflicted parents and friends. It will sting you to think that so many have been losers because of you, and that your parents, and brethren and sisters, have been so wasted and impoverished by your costly lusts; that you have given cause to all your wicked companions to curse the day that ever they knew you; and that you have filled so many other parents besides your own with grief and bitterness by infecting and defiling and debauching their children. I can hear all these saying to you, as Joshua said to Achan, "Ye have troubled us, but the Lord shall trouble you" (Joshua 7:25).

Last, I shall ask you this one question: What would you have your parents do with you? Their love makes them to be continually concerned for you, but they know not what to do with you; for all the means which they have yet used for your good have only aggravated your guilt and their grief. While they kept you at home, you broke all the good orders and rules of government in the family. At set times for meals and family worship, either your places were empty or filled with sin. You disquieted your parents, wasted the estate, defiled or disturbed your brethren and sisters, and troubled the house night and day. When they sent you to school, you played the truants, grieved and dishonored your masters, debauched your schoolfellows, and were a reproach and scandal to the school. If they sent you to be apprentices, you hated and wronged your masters, and were a plague to the family. If any of you were sent to the university, you were the hellions of the college, and the society was sick of you till it expelled and cast you out. If after all other means were used, your parents sent you to sea, the atheism and wickedness of some of the seamen did you more harm than all the wonders of

God in the deep waters did you good. So that you returned as if the sea had made you like itself, more raging and boisterous than before, insomuch that your miserable parents can do nothing but spend their days in mourning for your sins, praying for your salvation, laboring to patiently bear your ruin, and to be content to live and die the fathers and mothers of fools.

And now, children, I will take my leave of you, and shall leave you to the God with whom you have to do, and with whom you must have to do forever. He is the God who will plead the cause of His own name, honor, and of religion with you, and who will plead the cause of your distressed parents with you. He is a God whose wrath you can neither escape nor bear. There is a war between this God and you, and if you can make it appear that you are greater, wiser, stronger, and better than He, you may go on. But my design in all this discourse is to persuade you to believe, repent, and obey the gospel and so to make peace with God through Jesus Christ.

And for your encouragement, I assure you that the grace of God and the merits of Christ are as sufficient to save you from all your horrid abominations as if you were as innocent as when you were newborns. God, Christ, the angels, your parents, your friends, and all that saints are ready to rejoice in your conversion and salvation; and your iniquities shall never be mentioned against you. But upon your unfeigned turning to Him, God will (as He is represented in the parable of the prodigal son) meet you in mercy, fall on your necks and kiss you, and entertain you with all the blessings of the gospel, saying, "These My children were dead, and are alive; they were lost, and are found."